MARY WALKER
WEARS THE PANTS

THE TRUE STORY OF
THE DOCTOR, REFORMER,
AND CIVIL WAR HERO

Cheryl Harness

Illustrated by **Carlo Molinari**

Albert Whitman & Company
Chicago, Illinois

Library of Congress Cataloging-in-Publication Data

Harness, Cheryl.
Mary Walker wears the pants : the true story of the doctor, reformer, and Civil War hero
/ Cheryl Harness ; illustrated by Carlo Molinari.
p. cm.
ISBN 978-0-8075-4990-2 (hardcover)
1. Walker, Mary Edwards, 1832-1919–Juvenile literature. 2. Physicians–United States–Biography.
3. Women physicians–United States–Biography–Juvenile literature.
4. Suffragists–United States–Biography–Juvenile literature.
5. United States–History–Civil War, 1861-1865–Medical care–Juvenile literature.
6. United States–History–Civil War, 1861-1865–Women–Juvenile literature. I. Title.
R154.W18H36 2013 610.82–dc23 [B] 2012019531

The design is by Carol Gildar.
For more information about Albert Whitman & Company,
visit our web site at www.albertwhitman.com.

For my pants-wearing nieces,
Sara, Kate, Lindsey, Rachel, and Amy.—C.H.

Wherever she went, people talked.
"There's that Miss Walker."
"Didn't I read about her in the newspaper?"
"What's that fancy medal on her coat?"
"Why, that's the Medal of Honor, the highest military decoration a man can get."
"But she's a woman!" a child might have exclaimed. "And she's wearing PANTS!"

You see, in the 1800s women wore skirts and men wore pants. This was the natural, proper custom, but not for Mary. She and other brave dress reformers started wearing trousers so they could move more freely.

Oh, folks had heard whispers of such things, but they'd never EVER seen it! Not in clear, summer daylight on a public street!

"Scandalous!"

"Positively sinful!"

"Outrageous!"

But Mary Walker was used to upsetting people. Her parents taught her to think for herself, even if it meant going against the rest of the world.

In the 1800s, most believed that only men should vote, govern, and do the doctoring. Not Mary. She campaigned for equal civil rights for all men *and* women. And she went to medical school.

In 1855, Dr. Mary Edwards Walker, M.D., became one of the very first female physicians.

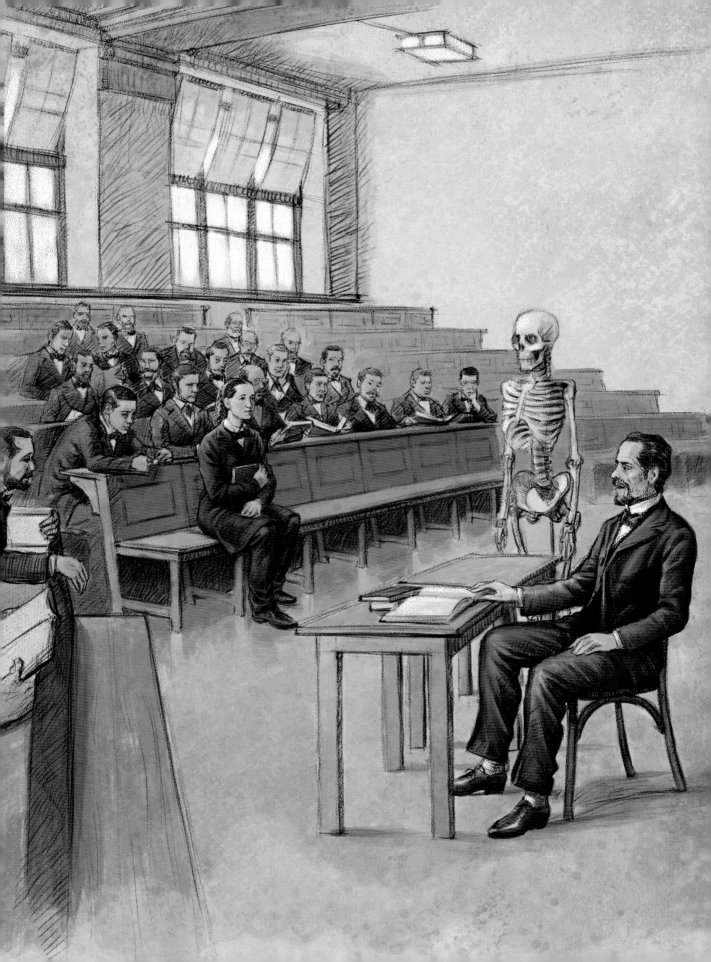

Many Americans, especially in the South, firmly believed that enslaving people from Africa was a normal thing to do. Not Mary. She agreed with other Americans, mostly in the North, who firmly opposed slavery. By 1860, Southerners decided to leave the United States and form their own nation, the Confederate States of America.

In the summer of 1861, the broad streets of Washington, D.C., were full of U.S. soldiers in blue uniforms. Many were still recovering from the first big fight of the war, a Confederate victory along Bull Run Creek in Virginia.

The president was worried and busy. Still, when Mr. Lincoln was out and about, he tipped his tall hat to ladies, who were trying to keep their long, wide hoopskirts from dragging through puddles, getting stepped on, or caught in wagon wheels.

Not Dr. Mary Walker. The nation was at war. This was no time to worry about skirts getting dirty. Many wounded soldiers had been brought to Washington, so Mary had come, too. She was going to help them.

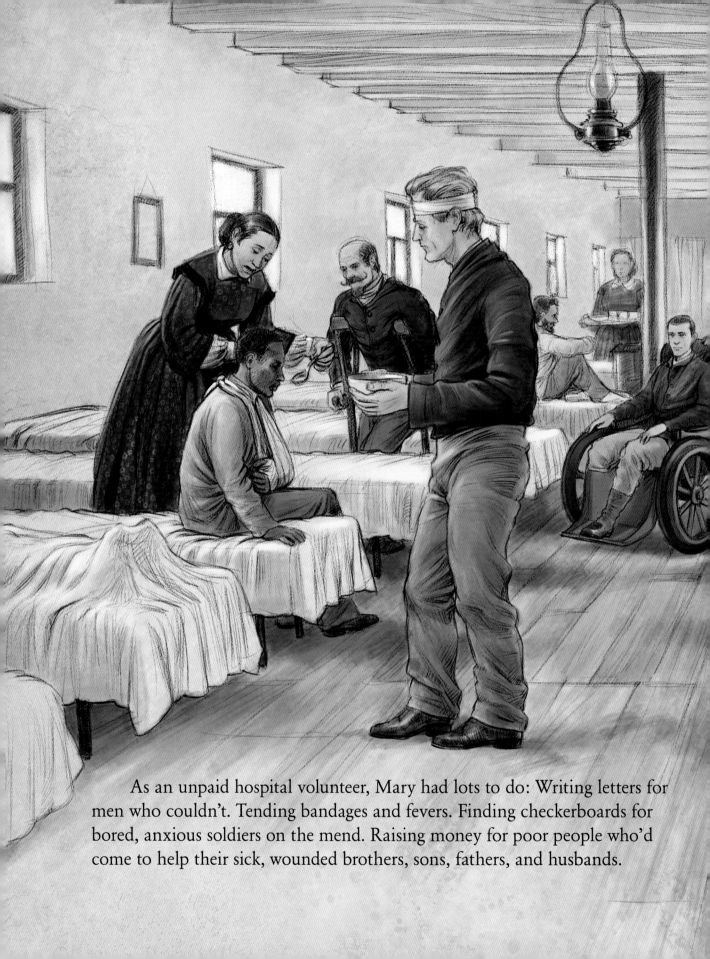

As an unpaid hospital volunteer, Mary had lots to do: Writing letters for men who couldn't. Tending bandages and fevers. Finding checkerboards for bored, anxious soldiers on the mend. Raising money for poor people who'd come to help their sick, wounded brothers, sons, fathers, and husbands.

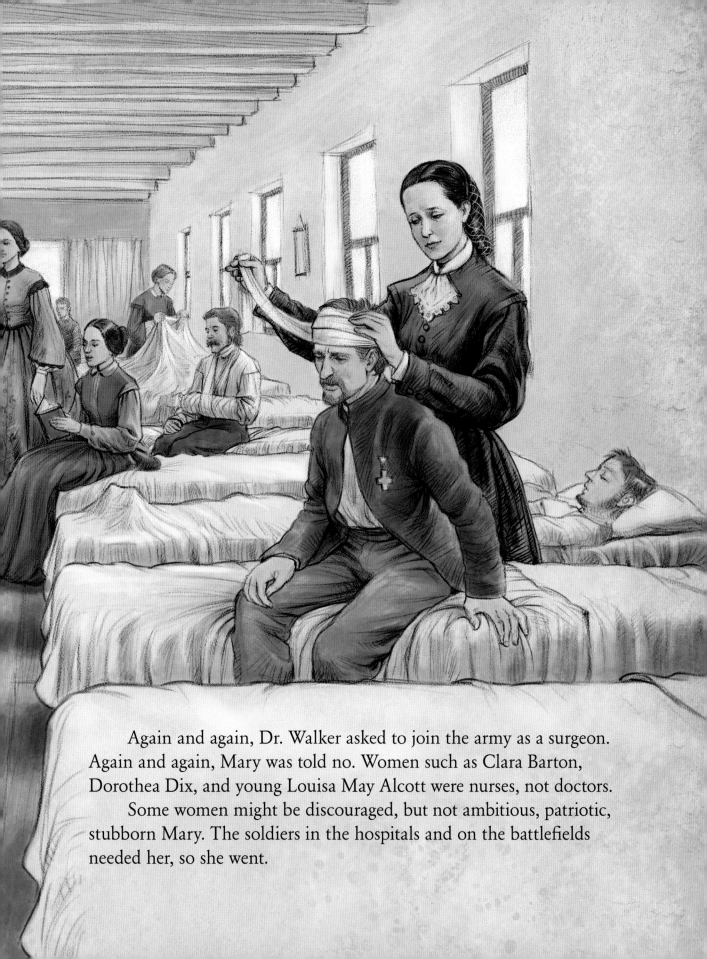

Again and again, Dr. Walker asked to join the army as a surgeon. Again and again, Mary was told no. Women such as Clara Barton, Dorothea Dix, and young Louisa May Alcott were nurses, not doctors.

Some women might be discouraged, but not ambitious, patriotic, stubborn Mary. The soldiers in the hospitals and on the battlefields needed her, so she went.

There were those who saw Mary as a pesky camp follower. But the war kept producing sick, shattered soldiers by the thousands and they needed care. Dr. Walker did her best to give it, no matter what the officers said, at field hospitals from Fredericksburg, Virginia, to Chattanooga, Tennessee.

She helped with medicines and bandages. When she thought that amputations were unnecessary, she tried to let soldiers keep their injured arms and legs. She gave the stretcher-bearers good advice, too: carry the wounded soldiers so their heads were higher than their feet.

At last, in late 1863, her work became official.
Major General George H. Thomas appointed her to
serve as an assistant surgeon in the U.S. Army—
a first for the military and a first for women.

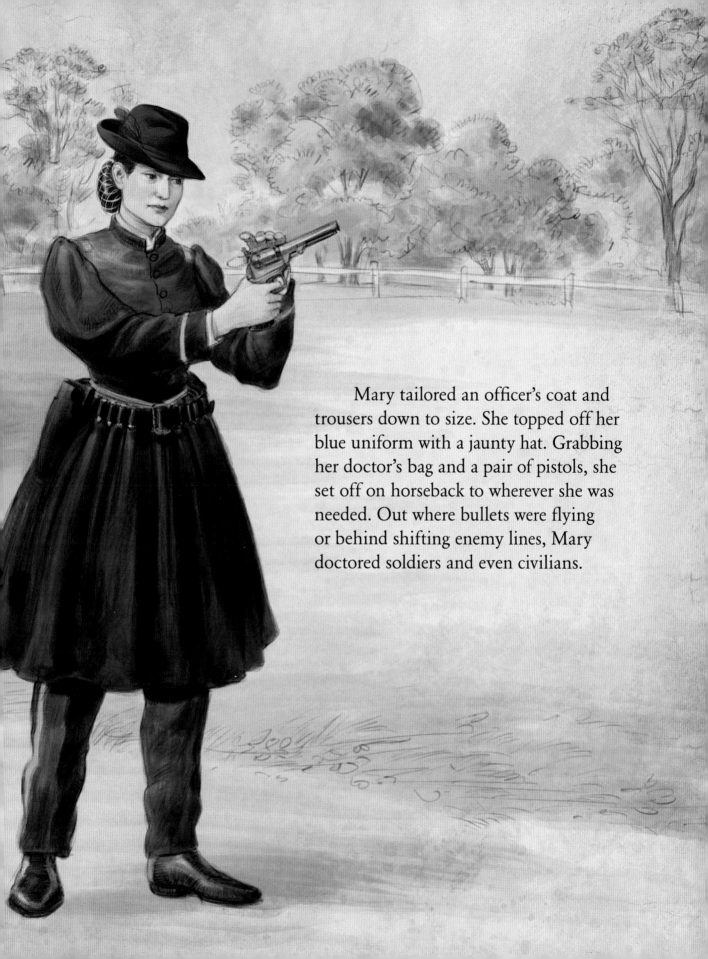

Mary tailored an officer's coat and trousers down to size. She topped off her blue uniform with a jaunty hat. Grabbing her doctor's bag and a pair of pistols, she set off on horseback to wherever she was needed. Out where bullets were flying or behind shifting enemy lines, Mary doctored soldiers and even civilians.

Most of her patients were U.S. fighters, but more than one fallen Rebel found himself being treated by the Yankee lady-surgeon. Dr. Walker went back and forth across enemy lines to help the wounded. Some people thought she was a spy and it is likely that this was true. Spying has always been a part of war.

On April 10, 1864, a Confederate sentry saw Mary, who was looking for wounded soldiers in Georgia, just south of the Tennessee border. He pointed his rifle at this strangely dressed woman. She had to be a spy!

"Halt!" he shouted.

Now Mary found herself on a train bound for Richmond, Virginia, the Confederate capital. She joined a thousand or so other U.S. prisoners of war, plus legions of rats and bugs, in "Castle Thunder," a warehouse that had been turned into a prison.

Throughout the spring of 1864, many thousands of men died in battle after battle not 75 miles from where Mary was imprisoned, wishing she could help them. In late summer, as U.S. forces were about to capture the South's important city of Atlanta, Georgia, officials worked out a deal: in exchange for the release of a Confederate surgeon, Dr. Walker would be let go. On August 12, Mary was free—and proud to have been exchanged an officer for an officer.

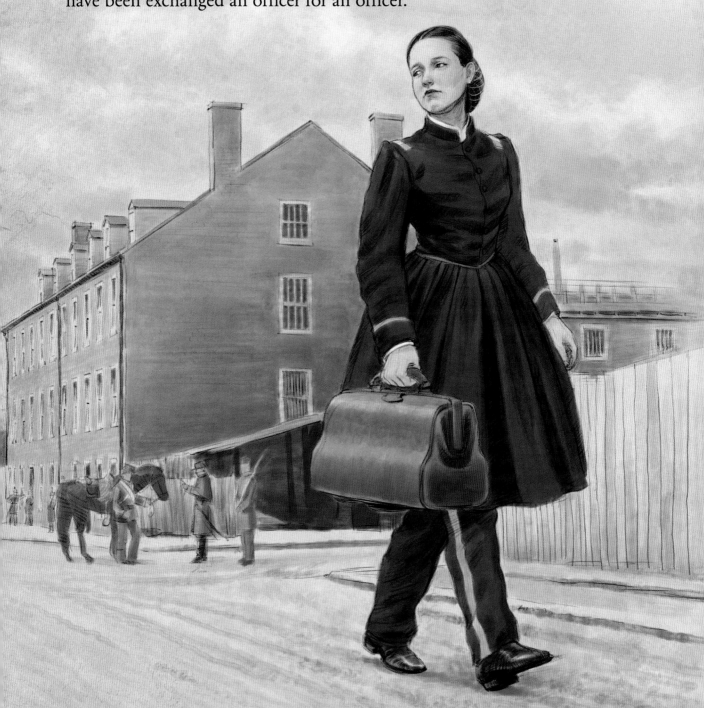

Dr. Walker hoped that she'd be sent back to the battlefields, but she was sent to look after female prisoners in Louisville, Kentucky. There, Mary also campaigned for President Lincoln's reelection in 1864. Then she cared for war orphans in Clarksville, Tennessee, where Mary celebrated the Union victory over the southern Confederacy. At last, in April 1865, the terrible Civil War was over.

On April 15, Mary and almost everyone else mourned the death of Abraham Lincoln, murdered by an assassin.

On July 4, 1865, Mary was back in bomb-blasted Richmond. Now she and other victorious Northerners were there to celebrate Independence Day. After the speeches and music, Dr. Walker stood on the steps of Virginia's state capitol in her splendid blue uniform. She read the Declaration of Independence to a crowd of Yankees and freed slaves. Defeated Rebels stayed indoors.

Then, like thousands of other war veterans, Mary went back home.

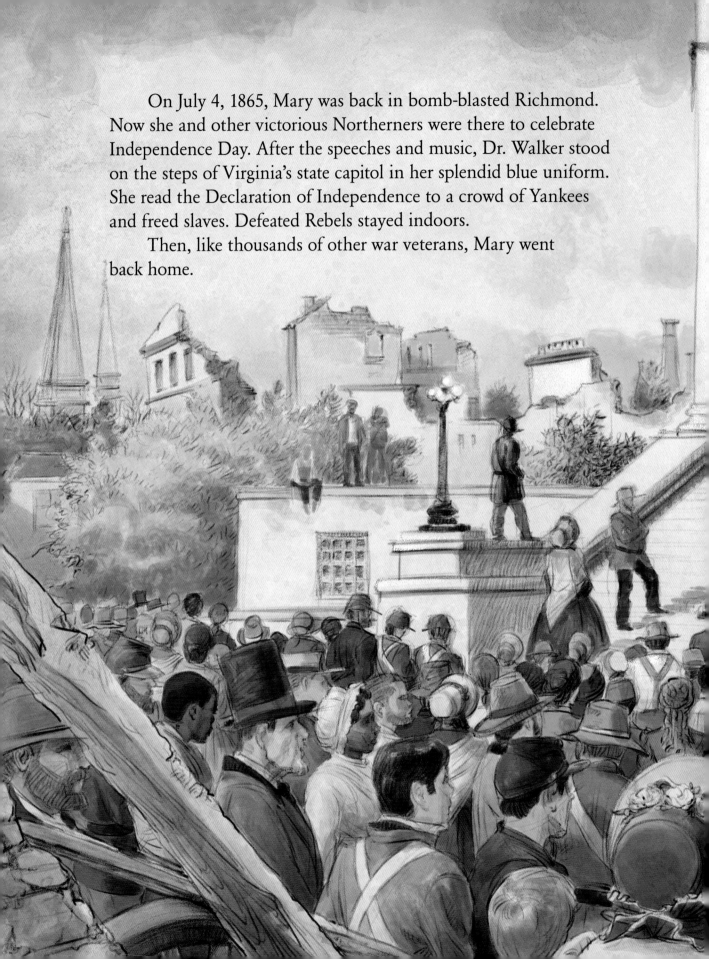

On January 24, 1866, Mary got a letter:

. . . Whereas in the opinion of the President an honorable recognition of her services and sufferings should be made:

It is ordered, That a testimonial thereof shall be hereby made and given to the said Dr. Mary E. Walker, and that the usual medal of honor for meritorious services be given her.

Given under my hand in the city of Washington, D.C., this 11th day of November, A.D. 1865.

Andrew Johnson, President
Edwin M. Stanton, Secretary of War

Countless courageous women had served their country, but none had *ever* had her valor so recognized.

After the war, audiences in America and abroad paid to hear Mary tell about her Civil War service and her imprisonment—and to see her in her notorious gentlemanly suit. It got her laughed at and made people angry. It caused scenes and even got her arrested! But Mary was stubborn and brave. It took courage for her to go to war—and to stay true to her ideals. As she said in 1866, "I wish it understood that I wear this style of dress from the highest, the purest and the noblest principle!"

But there was more to Mary than her trousers. She lived as she believed, as an individual, fully equal and entitled to walk, breathe, and think freely, unbound by a corset or her society's expectations.

Throughout the Civil War and the rest of her life, Dr. Mary Walker held fast to her convictions. She pinned her precious Medal of Honor to her manly suit coat and wore them both with pride.

Dr. Mary Edwards Walker was born November 26, 1832, in Oswego, New York. Her father, Alvah Walker, was a carpenter and a self-taught amateur physician. Mary worked as a teacher to pay for her classes at the Syracuse Medical School in New York. In 1855, she married fellow physician Albert Miller, and they set up an unsuccessful practice in Rome, New York. They separated in 1860, but their divorce was not finalized until 1869.

After two years of valiant volunteer work during the Civil War, her official field service began in late 1863. From April to August 1864, Mary was jailed. It amused the war-weary Confederates to make fun of their prisoner of war, who insisted on wearing such unwomanly clothing. In one of their newspapers, the *Richmond Whig,* Mary was described as a "deluded female" who was "by no means fair to look upon."

In 1866, Mary served as president of the National Dress Reform Association (NDRA). She was arrested that year, too: her pants attracted a crowd on a New York City street. But, like the women (and men) of the NDRA, Mary believed that females should be free to defy fashion and *not* wear breath-constricting corsets and long, movement-restricting skirts. Mary was proud of attracting attention to the NDRA. Its members shared her ideals, but unlike Mary, few were willing to face jail and ridicule. Political officials twice turned her down when she offered herself as a Democratic candidate for Congress. Still, her political work led to a job with the U.S. Department of the Interior from 1882 to 1883.

At heart, Mary was a crusader. She championed simple, liberating, healthy clothes for females as well as their right to vote, think, and live as fully equal human beings. She published her many views in books such as *Hit* (1871). She traveled and lectured, sometimes for very low pay. Between journeys, she lived at her family's farm in Oswego and tended to her neighbors' medical ailments. As she grew older, she continued to wear her suit and top hat, and did her best to ignore those who made fun of her—as many who didn't know of her heroic past did.

Despite her service as a surgeon in the 52nd Ohio Infantry Regiment and her time spent as a prisoner of war, it took 33 years of requests before Mary received the veterans' benefits to which she was entitled: a monthly $20. However, in 1917, the U.S. Congress ordered 84-year-old Mary, along with 910 other honorees, to return their Medals of Honor. The rules had been changed: the medal could only be awarded to those who'd been in "actual combat with the enemy," according to the revised standards. Mary flatly refused to give back her medal. She wore it all the remaining days of her life until she died on February 19, 1919, at the age of 86.

On August 20, 1920, less than a year after Mary died, the 19th Amendment to the Constitution was ratified, allowing female citizens the right to vote. In time, women went to the polls, wearing jeans, shorts, and all manner of pants. And, on June 10, 1977, President Jimmy Carter officially restored the Medal of Honor to Dr. Mary Edwards Walker.